A Note to Parents

DK READERS is a compelling program for beginning readers, designed in conjunction with leading literacy experts, including Dr. Linda Gambrell, Distinguished Professor of Education at Clemson University. Dr. Gambrell has served as President of the National Reading Conference, the College Reading Association, and the International Reading Association.

Beautiful illustrations and superb full-color photographs combine with engaging, easy-to-read stories to offer a fresh approach to each subject in the series. Each DK READER is guaranteed to capture a child's interest while developing his or her reading skills, general knowledge, and love of reading.

The five levels of DK READERS are aimed at different reading abilities, enabling you to choose the books that are exactly right for your child:

Pre-level 1: Learning to read
Level 1: Beginning to read
Level 2: Beginning to read alone
Level 3: Reading alone
Level 4: Proficient readers

The "normal" age at which a child begins to read can be anywhere from three to eight years old. Adult participation through the lower levels is very helpful for providing encouragement, discussing storylines, and sounding out unfamiliar words.

No matter which level you select, you can be sure that you are helping your child learn to read, then read to learn!

LONDON, NEW YORK, MUNICH,
MELBOURNE, and DELHI

Written by Fiona Lock

Series Editor Deborah Lock
U.S. Editor John Searcy
Art Editor Mary Sandberg
Production Editor Siu Chan
Production Pip Insley
Jacket Designer Mary Sandberg

Reading Consultant
Linda Gambrell, Ph.D.

First American Edition, 2008
11 12 13 14 15 14 13 12
Published in the United States by DK Publishing
375 Hudson Street, New York, New York 10014
016-DD448-04/2008

Copyright © 2008 Dorling Kindersley Limited

All rights reserved under International and Pan-American Copyright
Conventions. No part of this publication may be reproduced, stored
in a retrieval system, or transmitted in an form or by any means,
electronic, mechanical, photocopying, recording, or otherwise,
without the prior written permission of the copyright owner.
Published in Great Britain by Dorling Kindersley Limited

DK books are available at special discounts when purchased in bulk
for sales promotions, premiums, fund-raising, or educational use.
For details, contact:
DK Publishing Special Markets
375 Hudson Street
New York, New York 10014
SpecialSales@dk.com

A catalog record for this book
is available from the Library of Congress

ISBN: 978-0-7566-3749-1 (Paperback)
ISBN: 978-0-7566-3748-4 (Hardcover)

Color reproduction by Colourscan, Singapore
Printed and bound in the U.S.A. by Lake Book Manufacturing, Inc.

The publisher would like to thank the following for their kind permission to
reproduce their photographs:
a=above; b=below; c=center; l=left; r=right; t=top

Alamy Images: Image Quest Marine / Justin Peach 14br, 15bl, 15br; Michael
Moxter / Vario Images Gmbh & Co.kg 24-25; Dan Sullivan 30cl. **Corbis:**
Ralph Clevenger 27tr; Joe McDonald 18c; Rod Patterson / Gallo Images
19c. **DK Images:** Jerry Young 4c, 4cl, 4tr, 4-5b, 5br, 30fbl. **FLPA:** Michael &
Patricia Fogden / Minden Pictures 18tl. **Getty Images:** Norbert Wu / Science
Faction 24bl, 24br, 25bl, 25br. **naturepl.com:** Luiz Claudio Marigo 8t, 26c;
Mary McDonald 10-11, 32bl; Pete Oxford 9t, 14-15, 32cla; Tony Phelps
28c; Geoff Simpson 30cra. **Photolibrary:** Animals Animals / Earth Scenes
30cb, 31cb; Michael Fogden 12bl, 14bl; Mauritius Die Bildagentur Gmbh
28-29; Alastair Shay 13br, 32cl. **Photoshot / NHPA:** James Carmichael Jr
11t; Daniel Heuclin 17t; Image Quest 3-D 16-17. **Science Photo Library:**
Gregory Dimijian 13bl; S. R. Maglione 20-21; David M. Schleser / Nature's
Images 12-13. Jake Socha 27c. **Still Pictures:** Martin Harvey 31t.
FLPA: Gerry Ellis front jacket
All other images © Dorling Kindersley
For more information see: www.dkimages.com

Discover more at
www.dk.com

Contents

4 Scaly snakes

6 Rat snakes

8 Tree boas

10 Copperheads

12 Parrot snakes

14 Pit vipers

16 Rattlesnakes

18 Cobras

20 Pythons

22 Gaboon vipers

24 Sea snakes

26 Flying tree
   snakes

28 Horned vipers

30 Sleepy snakes

32 Glossary

DK READERS

LEARNING
pre-level
1
TO READ

Snakes
Slither and Hiss

DK Publishing

Hiss!
See the scaly snakes
slither here and there.

scales

5

Look out!

egg

rat snakes

This baby rat snake slides out of its egg. Hiss!

tree

tree boas

eye

Look out!
This tree boa keeps
its eyes open.
Hiss!

Look out!
This copperhead flicks
its tongue in and out.
Hiss!

copperheads

tongue

Look out!
This parrot snake opens
its jaws wider and wider.
Hiss!

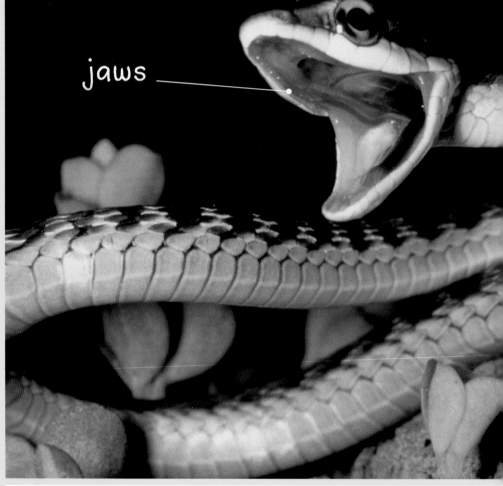

jaws

parrot snakes

Look out!
This pit viper bites
with its sharp fangs.
Hiss!

pit vipers

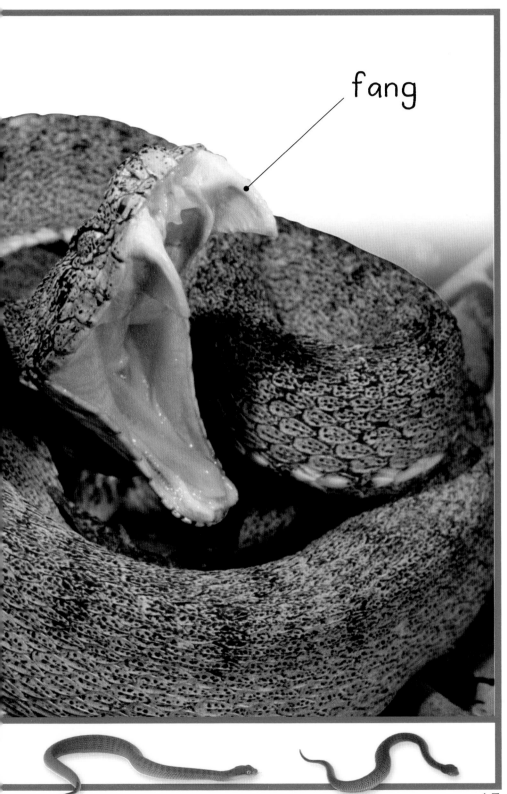

fang

Look out!
This rattlesnake
rattles its tail when
it is angry.
Rattle!

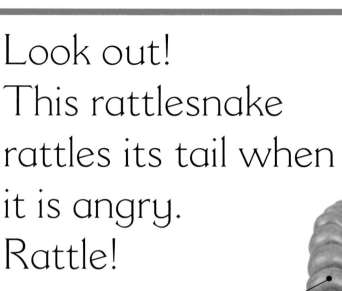

tail

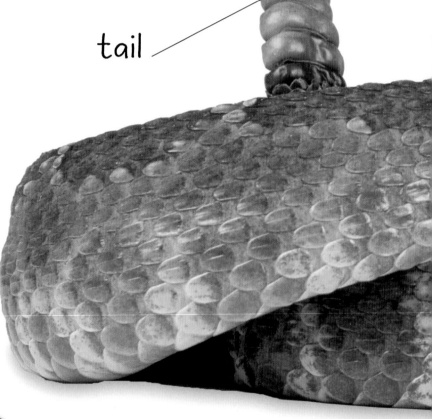

rattlesnakes

hood

cobras

Look out!
This cobra is getting
ready to spit.
Ssspit!

Look out!
This python wraps
around a rat and
squeezes tight.
Sssqueeze!

pythons

rat

Look out!
This gaboon viper
hides in the leaves.

 gaboon vipers

Ssssh!

leaves

snake

Look out!
This sea snake swims
this way and that.
Ssswish!

sea snakes

stripes

Look out!
This flying tree snake
glides from branch to
branch.
Hiss!

flying tree snakes

branch

body

Look out!
This horned viper winds
its way across the sand.
Hiss!

horned vipers

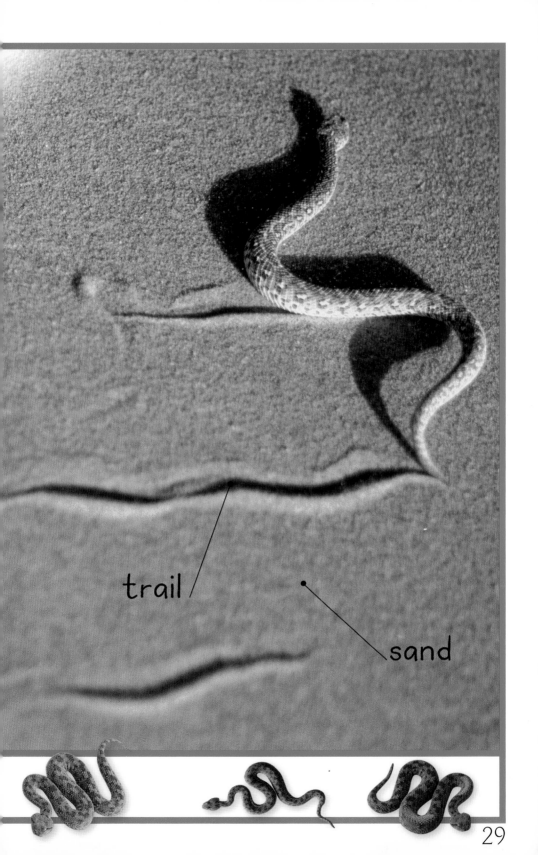

trail

sand

See the sleepy snakes
curl up in coils.
Ssssh!

 Can you slither

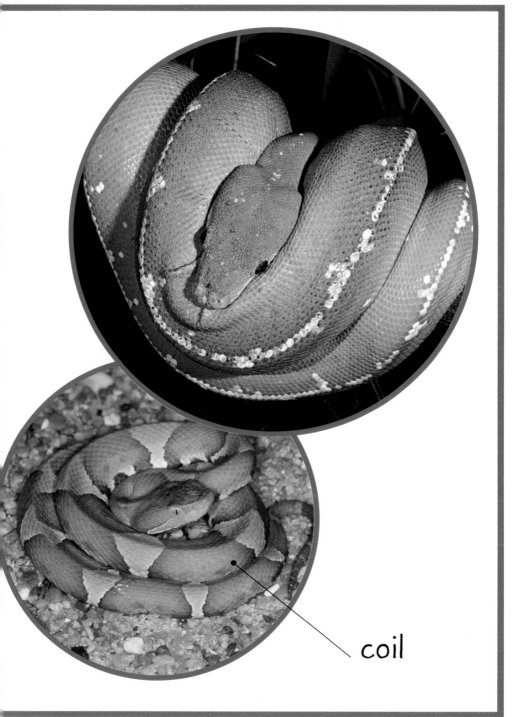

coil

and hiss like a snake?

Glossary

 **Egg** a soft, leathery shell with a baby snake growing inside

 **Fang** a large hollow tooth that shoots out poison

 **Jaws** bones that open and close the mouth

 **Scales** small, smooth plates that cover the skin

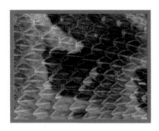 **Tongue** a mouth part that can smell, touch, and taste